FASHION DESIGN
FOR MODERNS

Rosalie Kolodny

FASHION DESIGN
FOR MODERNS

FAIRCHILD PUBLICATIONS, INC. NEW YORK

"An ancient fashion remains a curiousity,
a fashion but lately gone by becomes an absurdity,
a reigning mode, in which life stirs, strikes us
as the very personification of grace." O.U.

Acknowledgments are due to the many publications and individual photographers, artists and designers who have been so generous in giving permission for reprint. I also wish to express appreciation to the Fashion Institute of Technology Library and Nanice Crescioni for her kind assistance in facilitating research. I am especially grateful to the late Mr. Irving Grabois for his knowledgeable explanation of costs.

CONTENTS

FASHION, like all the arts, serves as a release from the humdrum in life. Part fantasy and part romance; it turned Cinderella into a princess and Beau Brummel into a legend. There are many "musts" in life; fashion not being one of them, and there is its pleasure.

To the designer, fashion is an art and more: it's also a business and an exciting, unpredictable one. Being a fashion designer means being aware of all the important new things that are happening around you. It's dashing off a simple little thing only to have it, to your amazement, break all records for sales. Fashion, like the theater, is a continual gamble, and working on a hit collection is as rewarding as being part of a hit play.

It's the down-to-earth aspects of fashion that we're concerned with in this short book—the ins and outs, the nuts and bolts of life in the world of fashion. We've tried to set down a designer's eye-view of the industry, from basics, such as a description of how a sample is made to more complicated matters, such as: what does a designer do when she needs fresh ideas? Incidentally, we've referred to the designer throughout the book as "she"—for the sake of simplicity and because, numerically, there are more women than men who are student designers.

FASHION DESIGN
FOR MODERNS

WHERE DOES THE DESIGNER WORK

MOST fashions made in America originate in one small area of one city: on Seventh Avenue, as the New York garment district is called. Two-thirds of all women's and children's clothes sold in the country are actually made there, or are designed by firms based there. Fashions are also designed and made in a few other large cities across the country—in Los Angeles, Minneapolis, St. Paul, St. Louis, and Dallas—but Mecca in the fashion world is New York.

Physically, the garment district is bounded by 34th and 40th Streets, extending from Sixth to Ninth Avenues. It's been estimated that it takes just 65 seconds to pass under it completely on the subway going from Penn Station to Times Square. Into this tiny area are crowded about 12,000 garment firms, literally hundreds to each block, in ancient lofts and modern skyscrapers. The streets are narrow and jammed with trucks and taxis; boys dodge in and out of the traffic pushing racks of bright-colored dresses. On a fine day, people pour out of the buildings at lunchtime and gather on the sidewalks to gossip about the business.

This, then, is the environment in which the fashion designer works. Her career begins the day she arrives on Seventh Avenue, portfolio in hand, to look for a job. This may be her first— or almost her first—real contact with the industry. She has already earned a degree in her field, has spent several years studying art history, fashion sketching, and draping, and she is ready now to test her talent on Seventh Avenue.

Approaching her first appointment, she finds herself riding up in an elevator in a tall building crammed in with an assortment of people, all cogs in the machinery that turns out fashion. Designers, a stream of buyers, chic models with huge carry-alls rushing to their next sample fitting appointments and a salesman or two who spend a large amount of time patiently riding up and down in elevators, as they go from building to building in the market, showing their lines of fabrics, or trimmings to designers.

The elevator opens on a view of showroom doors, the firm's name lettered above them. Entering, the young designer finds herself in a tiny lobby furnished with benches, plants, and statuary. She's announced by a receptionist to the person who will interview her—in this case, the firm's designer—and is then directed through the next room, the showroom, a long softly-lit room, with an attentive hush and thick, soft carpeting. There are mirrored walls and mutely-toned velvety drapes shielding doorways. Along one wall there are small tables that look rather 18th century, each flanked by a set of chairs; some are occupied now by buyers and the firm's salespeople.

The young designer is led directly from the

showroom (the lobby and offices that open off it are called the "front" of the firm) into the "back," to the sample room. The contrast between the front and the back is tremendous, like going backstage at the theater. The sample room (also called the designing room) is plain, drab, gray, with a bare concrete floor; crowded with cutting tables, sewing machines, dress forms, and people, a place of tremendous activity, compared to the decorous calm out front. The floor is littered with pins and bits of fabric. The designer steps into the room for the fitting,

trailed by an exquisitely made-up model in a sequined cocktail dress. Standing in the midst of the spilled pins and apparent chaos of the sample room, the model looks decidedly out of place.

The designer also works in a small office off the sample room, and it's here that the interview takes place. Her desk is buried under masses of inspirational material—sketches, fabric swatches, costume jewelry, bits of fur—and more of the same are pinned on the bulletin board above it. On shelves close by are bolts of the fabrics already chosen for the collection.

Geoffrey Beene showing for Spring '67.

THE JOB INTERVIEW

THE young design graduate stands now on the verge of her apprenticeship; she's looking for a position as a sketcher or possibly as an assistant designer. The names are misleading. The "assistant," as she's called in the language of Seventh Avenue, has a highly technical job; she doesn't design but cuts and supervises the making of samples. As the interpreter of the designer's ideas, she too must have a strong fashion feeling. Assistants sometimes eventually become designers, another route is from creative sketcher to designer.

If the graduate is looking for a job as a sketcher, the question uppermost in her mind during the interview is: what kind of sketcher does the firm want? Some designers expect their sketcher to double as a secretary—errand girl, giving her little responsibility; others want a creative sketcher, someone who will contribute ideas to the collection and will work closely with the designer in developing it. In either case, the sketcher's main job is to make formal drawings from the designer's rough ones; the drawings are kept in a binder as a permanent record of the collection, and they're also used by the assistant in cutting patterns.

The designer judges the applicant both on the basis of her portfolio, and also on her appearance. In no other field is the appearance of the job applicant so important—especially for a woman. What she wears, her make-up, her hair, all express what she knows about fashion. Her portfolio contains sketches of her own designs and if it's a good one, it strikes a nice balance between those that are new-looking, but saleable and fashions that are daringly experimental.

The sketches are of designs for the season after the current one; a designer looking for a job in early spring, for instance, (the summer collection has been shown) comes prepared with sketches of fall fashions.

Besides her portfolio and appearance, the applicant is judged on the experience she's had, if she's had any; connections and luck have never been deterrents to landing a job, either. It also helps if she knows something about the workings of the industry: about how samples are made and how a collection evolves.

The interview may or may not result in a job offer, but the graduate should be aware, at the outset of her job-hunting, that a career in design means hard work and a fair share of headaches, in addition to all the potential rewards. Some beginners will hold out for a job in a particular specialty . . . others will begin where they can, hopeful of moving into their preferred field later on. But in any case the young designer should give some consideration to what *kind* of fashion she wants to design. Almost all garment firms specialize: they make a particular type of fashion in particular price and size ranges. We're concerned in this book mostly with firms which make sportswear, street wear, coats and suits and evening wear, (but there are also, of course, manufacturers of bathing suits, sleepwear, lingerie, ski clothes, furs, children's wear, and men's wear).

The Bustle (1870's).

SOME NOTES ON SIZING

FIRST, *some notes on sizing:* Size ranges are divided by figure types; miss (or missy) for the average figure, junior for the shorter smaller proportioned young woman, petites for of course the petite figure even smaller than junior, women's sizes for the average heavier woman, and the half size range for the shorter, heavier woman. At the beginning of this century there were thought to be only two basic figure types; the matronly, heavy waisted, heavy bosomed housewife and the wasp waisted, high bosomed shorter woman of leisure. Women's sizes fitted the former, misses the latter. Most ready-to-wear in those days anyway were two piece affairs where waistline proportions weren't of too much concern. The skirt was hiked up to meet the waistline wherever it might be. As women gained their freedom and began to lead a variety of lives, it became apparent, a variety of figures needed to be fitted. This may have happened because the female figure was going through a process of evolution. Sports created a woman of leisure with a longer torso, new knowledge of nutrition created a slimmer figure, (Sizes back in cavewomen days for

instance, would have ranged from mammoth to extra mammoth, while for the colonial lady in the New World and her counterpart in continental Europe in the same era, proportions were tiny, equal to today's Junior Petite—the human body *does* change) or it may have been a growing sophistication about sizing itself. In any case, most garment firms today specialize in one size range and high fashion is usually found in the misses sizes, 6 to 16. For example, a garment firm may finally be defined as a maker of career girl coats and suits in misses sizes with prices wholesaling from $23.75 to $39.75.

It's desirable, though not always possible, for a designer to start out with the kind of firm that makes the kind of fashion she's interested in, because it will be difficult for her once she's established, to transfer to another type of firm, although it has been done. (Several successful New York designers have spent their early career years going from one position to another designing for various kinds of fashion houses.) Eventually though, someone whose experience is all in sportswear, for example, will find it difficult to switch

Mrs. Gould,
turn of the century.

to a firm that makes evening wear, if she finally decides it's evening fashions she's interested in. The price level makes a difference, too: a designer of higher-priced fashions can almost always shift to a lower-priced house if she wants to, but it's hard to move in the other direction. Consequently, someone who feels she can only be happy designing high fashion should probably hold out for a job with a higher-priced house.

Most of the glamor and prestige in the fashion world go to the couture designers—those who design high fashion, set a trend in fashion, and are copied by other designers. To be a couturier, a designer needs special talents: originality, plus a kind of sixth sense that helps her spot a new direction in fashion even before it has come into being. It's almost uncanny, the way so many couturiers in different countries will develop the

The Natural Look (1965).

same trend at the same time. This sixth sense seems to be something inborn: either a designer has it, or she doesn't. If she doesn't, but she has talent and good taste, she may never become a couturier: however, she can still be a good commercial designer, following along on trends other people have launched.

There's more status, of course, in being a high fashion designer, but there's a different challenge to be found in the lower-priced market and a different kind of reward. The challenge is to create good fashion from inexpensive materials; the reward, to know that literally thousands of women are wearing something you designed. Hundreds of designers in low-priced houses today are making exciting, inexpensive fashions, and they've made the American garment industry famous around the world for just that.

[25]

Gaston Berthelot
of Dior, New York.

HOW
SAMPLES
ARE MADE

Rudi Gernreich at work.

THE basic unit of a designer's collection is the sample garment. Each sample begins with an idea in the designer's mind. Sometimes the idea arrives full-blown and she sketches it immediately; sometimes it evolves through a series of sketches, or it comes to her as she drapes fabric experimentally on a model. There are designers who work mostly by sketching, others who work by draping, and still others who do both.

When an idea is put into work, the designer makes a rough drawing, and her sketcher turns it into a more formal one and passes it on, with a swatch of the fabric the designer believes is right for the style, to the assistant. Working from the drawing, the assistant develops a muslin pattern,

draping it as she goes along on a dress form. When she has finished, a model is called in, and the designer and the assistant work together to fit the muslin. They go through endless amounts of discussion: about silhouette, fit, and—very important—fabric. The model is asked to walk away, turn, and come back, so that the designer can see the style in motion. The questions she asks herself and her assistant are "Does it look young?" and "Does it look new?" The trend to young-looking clothes has grown in America over the years, until saying that a design looks "old" is the worst thing you can say about it—except, perhaps, to point out that it looks like last season.

The muslin is fitted and refitted and the de-

[29]

Bill Blass in his sample room.

signer experiments freely with it; she may change the design or fabric radically. When at last she is satisfied, the style is put into work. The assistant perfects her pattern, cuts it in the fabric that's been decided on, and passes it on, with minute instructions, to a sample hand.

Sample hands are highly skilled workers; they drape and construct the sample garments. Each one has her own dress form, an exact duplicate of the fitting model, and the designer's work sketch is usually pinned somewhere on her sewing machine. Each is responsible for one and a half to two garments a week, so with six or eight sample hands to supervise, plus fittings, the assistant is kept busy. A finisher helps the sample hands, sewing on snapfastners and hooks, hemming samples, and generally making herself useful. In time, she may become a sample hand herself. Firms that make only coats and suits employ tailors instead of sample hands; firms that make dresses as well as coats and suits employ both tailors and sample hands.

After the sample hand has made up the garment in basted form, there's another fitting on the model; this is called the first basted fitting. Here, again, the designer takes a hand and important changes may be made, in fact, the dress may be completely dismantled at this point and started over—and it can still turn out to be one of the best numbers in the collection. The sample is checked closely for proper fit now; on opening day every seam must look absolutely perfect. The same questions are asked again: Is the style young? Is it new? The designer hopes to follow the same important fashion trends other houses (especially more expensive houses) are following; but to persuade buyers to make their choices from her collection, rather than from the others, she has to offer something special, something very fresh-looking. She must also keep a balance between what's new and what's wearable and beautiful. The special, distinctive features she decided on for her collection may be very small things: for

instance, in one season, she may adapt square armholes for her sleeveless dresses.

After the fitting, corrections are made, and then there's a second basted fitting to check. If it goes well, the sample is then stitched and finished by the sample hand, except for last fittings when final decisions are made as to the hemline, sleeve-length, and possibly trimming.

In some designing rooms, assistants aren't used and all sample patterns and cutting are done by the individual sample hands. In other small firms, the designer may do her own work and that of the assistant as well.

A Gernreich fitting.

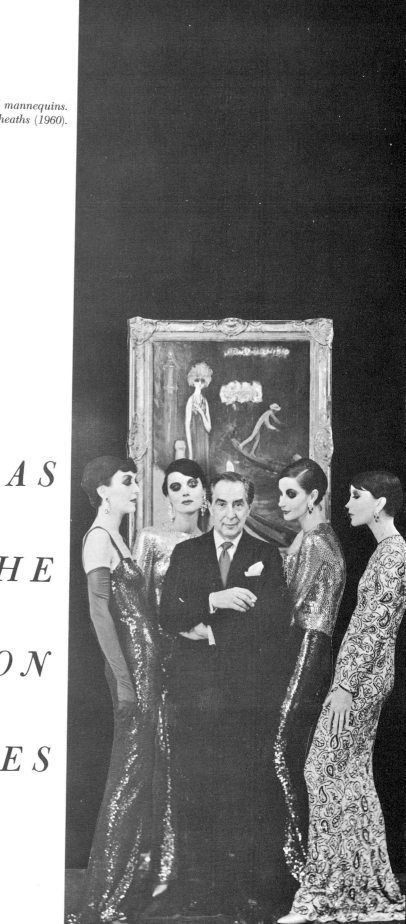

Norman Norell and mannequins.
Sequin sheaths (1960).

AS

THE

COLLECTION

EVOLVES

THERE's a regular rhythm to the designer's life, starting with the pleasant lull that occurs between collections, which lasts from one to three weeks, and building up gradually, as the new collection develops, to a climax at the next opening when life may become absolutely frantic. (Sometimes samples have to be shown basted together—and they can still turn out to be the best in the line.

Most of the time, the designer is kept quite busy, planning the collection and checking fittings on models. She keeps a steady stream of sketches going into work, and she must also take time out to look at lines of fabrics, buttons, embroidery, pleating, flowers, jewelry, and so on; she checks these for inspiration, and to find finishing touches for samples in work.

Upper-priced firms that make afternoon and evening wear generally show three to five collections a year: fall, resort, holiday, spring, and summer; sometimes collections are combined. Designers often have a favorite season, one collection they enjoy designing more than they do the others. The spring collection is usually the smallest, though it hasn't always been; spring in the Northeast has been much shorter in recent years than it was in the past, and fashion collections reflect this meteorological change. Summer lines have changed, too; they're geared now both to hot weather and to air-conditioned places— providing hosts of dresses with light cover-ups to be worn indoors.

Work on a collection begins four to six months before the shipping date and the opening takes place approximately three months before shipping. The designer first spends days, sometimes weeks, going around to fabric houses, examining and selecting fabrics, before she begins to structure her collection. Because fabrics are a complicated subject, we will return to them later. The designer must decide, to begin with, how large the complete collection will be. In an up-

Norell's 1920's Look (Fall '65).

Norell Sequin Gown.

The Ruffle Evolution.
Bill Blass (1961) (1965).

Bill Blass Ruffles, '64.

Norell Sequin Pajamas, Fall '66.

per-priced house, for the average fall collection—
always the largest of the year—she designs from
110 to 135 samples; she estimates that, after discards, there will be 85 to 90 left. Smaller firms,
and those not so well established, have smaller
collections.

The variety of clothes the collection covers
increases as the price goes up and high fashion
becomes more important. Lower-priced firms are
often quite specialized, while a high-priced house
may make everything from sportswear to evening
wear. In these wide-ranging collections, samples
are usually shown in groups separated by time of
day. Therefore, a show might start with casual
wear, go on to afternoon dresses, cocktail, and
then evening fashions. The evening gowns are
the showpieces of the collection and are always
good for a round of applause. Firms with a
smaller range might group into day, afternoon, and
cocktail fashions, while the house that makes
only daytime fashions will group by fabric: wools,
knits, novelties, and so on. The designer must be
cautious as she works and not go overboard by
making too many designs in any one group; her
completed sketches are a record of progress and
will tell her at a glance what she needs to fill
out the line in design and fabric.

Once she's really underway, the designer works
out a theme for her collection. The theme may
evolve quite naturally from one exciting idea—
or the designer may have a theme in mind before
she starts the collection. It may be a new idea
shown in a number of ways so that by sheer
emphasis it becomes identified as her own—for
instance, Norell one season featured jumpers
throughout his collection, (and the "Norell
jumper" was quickly copied by other houses).
Sometimes, there's a separate theme for each
group within the collection. A fabric the designer believes in may be emphasized, or a
color or color combination; or these may be
strewn throughout the collection.

Most couture houses include something that is

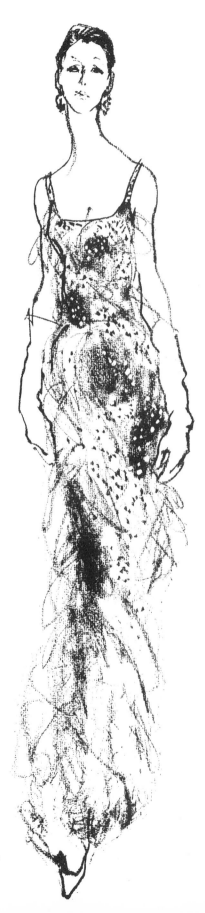

More Norell Sequins Evolve.

St. Laurent's Fisherman Smock 1962 version.

Next Page, Left; St. Laurent's '65 version.

characteristic of the designer of the firm. Trigère, for example, is known for capes, Chanel for her suits, and Grès for magnificent sculptured jersey gowns. These signature fashions always have something fresh about them, with each collection. Another example, is Norell's famous sequined evening sheaths; in his fall, 1964, collection, he made them again with coq feather hems and they looked very new. The Fall 1965 version was shown short, in the flapper silhouette of the Twenties and for Fall 1966, he designed sequined pajamas.

Top designers rarely make a really basic change in the kind of fashion they show; if they did, they might scare away old customers. Most established firms know precisely who their customers are; for instance, one designer may cater to women who dislike anything extreme; another, to young women who want high fashion. Stores (or departments within stores) often specialize in the same way.

As the collection develops, it is important for the designer to keep her price range firmly in mind. She must consider everything that goes into each sample—fabric, trimming, labor, and so on. There are moments when lush embroidery is difficult to resist, but if it takes the garment out of a saleable price range, it must be at least modified. A top-notch designer is up on costs, even for the minor ingredients. Though she can't be completely accurate in her estimate, she does her best, so that there will be less substitution in the production stage. Otherwise, she may not even recognize the garment as it's being shipped, and buyers will be disappointed. Costs are discussed in detail on pages 68–69.

As in all creative jobs, there are some days when the designer looks at her work and every

The Famous Trigère Capes

dress looks like a "dog"; the collection may be nearly finished and a glance through it makes her feel slightly sick. On other days, everything she's done looks like fashion news.

It's easy for a designer to lose her perspective while she's doing a collection. She has to absorb what's new and know what to do with it, and at the same time she must take care not to over-do a new trend. If she's not careful, she may turn out a collection that is creative, but sadly short on good, wearable, saleable styles; or she may go overboard in the other direction, become too cautious, and do nothing but bread-and-butter numbers (though some firms do well with a purely bread-and-butter line). Occasionally, she may reach a point where she can't see the collection as a whole anymore, and she loses her sense of direction. Usually, though, her unconscious keeps her on the track, even when she feels she's off it.

THE COLLECTION
HAS A TRIAL RUN

*Figuring
sample costs;
Henry Sherman,
president of
Dior, New York.*

THE preview—a kind of trial run before the show—takes place when the collection is in its final stages, with just a few last samples left in the work. At this time, the designer takes advantage of the experience and intuition of the people she works with. She also girds for battle. Her critics are the designing, sales, and production staffs of the firm.

The samples are modeled one at a time in the showroom. Each is discussed thoroughly from the points of view of saleability and price; the discussion is informal, but the manufacturer has the final say about which samples will become part of the collection. High fashion samples that may not sell in quantity, but add flair to the collection are often retained; since they reflect new fashion trends, they can be used for magazine photographs.

Some styles, inevitably, become discards, and, inevitably, some of these are the designer's favorite "babies." Occasionally, she fights for a sample she believes in, maintaining that the other members of the firm don't understand it because it's too new. If she wins her battle she may in the long run turn out to be right—or again, she may not. Once the collection is shown, it's the store buyers who have the last word.

All designers eventually have to come to grips with the hard facts of fashion: that every design must be judged by whether or not it will sell, and that a style that's new and exciting is not necessarily saleable. The designer must learn to take the commercial view of her own work.

However, in some cases, it's best for a designer to fight a long, quiet, but stubborn fight for what she believes in. A really good designer can modify or sometimes even change the kind of fashion her firm makes: can gradually introduce a younger, fresher, more imaginative look.

The ability to judge what will sell and what won't is vital, of course, to the firm's survival. Still, every collection has its surprises. Recently, a successful designer showed a wool ensemble—a very simple dress with a jacket—that sold rather mildly in the showroom; but after it was shipped to stores hundreds of reorders for the dress alone poured in from all over the country; there were even more reorders later, until thousands had been shipped. Apparently, women found the dress flattering. It was made in fashionable colors, had a lovely shape, and looked well with jewelry. Samples like this are "sleepers;" their potential unsuspected, one reason fashion is such an unpredictable, and exciting field.

During the preview, final decisions are made on the groupings within the collection. Also final decisions on accessories to be worn with each style are selected. At this time, the designer works with a nucleus of models; models are hired by the hour and they're expensive, so just a few are used for the original fittings. Additional girls with the same measurements are brought in from agencies for the formal showings. A firm sometimes keeps one model as a permanent employee. At the preview, and again just before the showing, the designer checks the samples on the models, tries and retries them to make sure each is worn by the girl it suits the best. Designers all have their favorite models, girls they use over and over again.

The final chore before the opening is the decision on color ranges. Most firms ship each style in three or four different colors. The designer, working with swatch books provided by the fabric houses, picks for each sample colors she believes are attractive, saleable, and fashionable for the coming season. These are then given descriptive names, such as Persian pink, Amalfi violet.

After the preview, a date is picked for the opening, and invitations are sent out to buyers. They attend the showing either on opening day or on one of the follow-up days; usually, the collection is shown for two weeks.

A Gernreich Showing.

THE BIG QUESTION ON OPENING DAY: DID THEY WRITE?

O<small>N OPENING DAY</small> the showroom is transformed into a small theater filled with rows of small gilt chairs, each bearing a pad and pencil. As the hour approaches, buyers begin to drift in and sit waiting for the show to begin.

Behind the curtain in the models' dressing room, there's a nervous flutter of excitement. The assistant and the sketcher dart back and forth, lining up accessories, checking last-minute details in tense whispers:

"Where are the orange gloves? I'm sure I had them. I've *got* to find the orange gloves."

The models sit in front of their mirrors, making up. The samples are hung on a rack in groups, and each group has a name above it— "Pat," "Virginia"—the names of the models who will wear the dresses. There are great bins full of hats, and gloves and jewelry are laid out in neat rows on a table.

The designer peers anxiously through a gap in the curtains to see if the notables of the buying world have arrived yet. The showroom is decked with plants and flowers; the chairs are filling up. The tension is all behind the curtain, and from there the buyers in the audience look blissfully calm and comfortable.

At last, the narrator steps through the curtain and addresses the audience and the show begins. A model glides across the room; she turns, pauses and starts back. She wears a thick tweed suit muffled in fur. Outside the air-conditioned showroom it's late May and the thermometer is edging toward the eighties. The narrator finishes her description, the model steps back through the door into the dressing room, and in the same breath the next girl emerges.

Out on the floor, the models are ice-cool and elegant. The minute they re-enter the dressing room, bedlam breaks loose as the model's dresser leaps to help her out of one outfit and into another.

In the showroom, the buyers watch intently.

Backstage with Donald Brooks.

For them, this is a moment of truth. They rely on experience to tell them which styles will sell and which won't; the right choices now can make the difference later between a good season and a disappointing one. Each buyer tries for a poker face, won't flicker as much as an eyelash even when a model glides by wearing something he recognizes as a real "Ford." His object is to conceal his orders from his competitors.

The designer's eyes keep wandering to the pads and pencils in the buyers' hands, eager to catch numbers being jotted down. The manufacturer watches too; if it's a small enough firm, he'll feel the flush of a good collection, or the pinch of a poor one, in his own pocket.

The showpieces of the collection are saved for last and as the models exit the designer listens for the applause. An enthusiastic audience doesn't

guarantee a successful collection, but it's a very encouraging sign. As soon as the show is over, she corners one of the firm's salesmen. "Did they write?" she asks anxiously. When buyers feel a collection is unsaleable they don't bother to note numbers down.

Now the firm's salespeople wheel the clothes out on racks for the buyers to examine more closely. The final verdict on a collection isn't in until all the reorders have been totaled up months later, but if the line is very good buyers may start handing in their orders right after the show, to be sure of getting what they want. But in most cases they go away without committing themselves, look at other lines, and eventually come back to review what they saw and leave their orders.

The manufacturer doesn't know how much

Opening Day at Bill Blass'.

A last-minute review. Trigère in the dressing room.

fabric to cut until all the orders are in. Not every style he has shown will stir enough interest to be worth cutting; he'll feel encouraged if, out of a hundred styles, he eventually has enough orders to put, say sixty-six into production. As show follows show for the two weeks the collection is on view, it becomes obvious that some numbers are failures, and they are quietly dropped from the line. The mortality rate for samples is greatest during the period of the showings.

There's a saying on Seventh Avenue—borrowed from films—that you're only as good as your last collection. As in the theater, a line can be a hit or a flop or it may fall somewhere in between. A well-seasoned designer may not produce a hit every time, but she can usually be sure of a moderate success. New designers sometimes suffer through a flop or two while they're learning. One or two runners can carry a line, just as one

actor can sometimes carry an otherwise-poor play; however, the precise characteristics that make a number a runner (it's also called a Ford) can't be pinned down; there's no ready-made formula. If there were, every collection would be a solid hit.

Many firms, after the opening, put the show on the road. Segments of the collection are flown to Los Angeles, Chicago, Dallas, and other big cities; someone from the firm's sales staff accompanies them. At each stopover, buyers from local stores come to see the collection shown on local models, and to place orders.

Most of the firm's profits are from reorders, and if a line really catches on, the manufacturer may not be able to handle all the reorders that flood in; however, he can always farm out what he can't cope with, to outside contractors.

ABOUT RUNNERS AND GOOD HANGER DRESSES

Early version of Chanel Suit, 1929.

1967

1958

1962

The Classic Runner:
The Chanel Cardigan Suit.

Eᴠᴇʀʏ successful firm occasionally hits a runner or Ford; a garment that sells from the minute it arrives· in the stores and is reordered in great quantities. A more expensive dress house may receive 1,000 reorders; a low-price house, 10,000 or more. This, of course, is the designer's dream. It's delightful to walk down Fifth Avenue and come across three or four women all wearing the same dress, if you're the person who designed it.

When the season ends, in the normal course of events, reorders stop. However, good dresses, like old soldiers, never really die; they fade gently away, reappearing for several seasons with their silhouette or fabric changed to conform to current trends, but retaining whatever feature it was that made them so desirable. A good dress that lasts several seasons adds greatly to the firm's profits and the designer's prestige. The Chanel suit is a classic example of a lasting style.

What about a sample that looks magnificent on a model at the opening, but because of complex construction loses appeal when on a hanger. Buyers know that when a garment hangs clumsily it doesn't arouse the customer's interest; she hasn't seen it on a model, and she probably won't even bother to try it on unless she is persuaded by a salesperson or unless the buyer believes in it and displays it well. The rule of thumb is: chances of success are greater if the garment looks well on the hanger.

*At
the races Chanel suit—
Paris
1927.*

*Checking
a duplicate.*

THE

DESIGNER'S WORK

DOESN'T END

WITH THE

OPENING

AFTER the collection has been shown, a pattern-maker sets to work to turn the successful samples into paper patterns cut to standard sizes. He first makes a copy in muslin, then turns this into a flat pattern, which is sent to the factory where a test duplicate is made. Then comes a comparative fitting: the duplicate, worn by a duplicate model, is checked against the original sample, worn by a showroom model.

Showroom models have off-size figures. Usually, they're size 10 through the shoulders, size 8 at the hips, they have very long waists and are taller than average. Duplicate models have standard-size figures. They're not used at the showing because the clothes look more dramatic on the tall, lean showroom girls.

Some firms rely completely on a production man to check out the duplicates, but most at this stage want the advice of the designer and her assistant. For the designer, it's advisable to be present at the fitting of the duplicate for several reasons. To begin with, there's the personal satisfaction of knowing that the garments shipped look as much like the original sample as possible.

Also, dresses that retain the fashion flair of the sample reorder better—and most of the firm's profits come from reorders. The best-designed collection won't be reordered if it's poorly produced or if there are too many substitutions in embroidery, lining, and so on.

As the duplicate is checked against the sample, the designer may find she needs to correct the shape of a collar or the hang of a skirt. Trying for a dramatic new look, she may have made her original sample with a very low neckline or experimented with a trend-setting length; but to make the style more saleable, buyers will often ask for small modifications. Even without buyers' requests, the pattern-maker makes changes as he works. Some are necessary; however, unless the pattern-maker has a strong feeling for fashion, a lot can be lost in the translation from sample to duplicate and from the individually-made dress to the factory-made.

After much work, (sometimes three or four duplicates have to be made) a duplicate is finally approved and the pattern is graded into sizes and cut into stock.

[57]

THE PEOPLE
THE DESIGNER
WORKS WITH

O NE OF the remarkable things about any garment firm is the melting pot atmosphere that's so characteristic of the industry. The Seventh Avenue designing room, the heart and soul of the better fashion industry is a world all its own. Designer, assistant, sample hands, tailors and models are all part of the team in the development of the new collection. All have a good fashion sense and can appreciate what the designer is trying to do as someone outside the garment world can't. Theirs is a constant shared struggle for creative perfection and beautiful fit. There's no stratification in the designing room, and when it comes to fashion all share the same language.

The piece-goods man: He handles orders for fabrics, both for the factory and for the sample room. His domain is a room lined with deep shelves, on which bolts of fabric are stacked.

The trimming woman (or man): She supplies everything from mundane hooks and eyes to jewelry, flowers, and furs. She orders for the factory and for the designing room, and she sets up appointments for the designer with salesmen who want to show lines of belts, flowers, buttons, furs, and so on.

The production man: He supervises all factory production, settles the labor prices of garments with the union and prices the sample collection. The designer often works with him and the pattern-maker to correct the duplicate of the sample so the corrected pattern can be graded into sizes and put into production.

The manufacturer: He usually heads his sales staff; sometimes production. Like the producer in the theater, the manufacturer takes a risk. The success of his business depends on collections that sell and reorder well. The designer's job is to design a saleable collection; the manufacturer's is to have the acumen to pick a good designer. It's up to the novice designer to ask what she feels is a fair price for her skills. When she's proven successful, most manufacturers will pay top salary, for there is more assurance of profit on their investment.

In a sense, the designer is in business for herself; she develops a reputation in the fashion field and this has a monetary value. Just as some works of art sell for $100 and some for $150,000, designers' incomes vary widely. With an established, higher-priced firm, the designer makes an excellent salary—but of course she didn't "arrive" overnight; she started somewhere as an assistant or sketcher, working for other designers to accumulate experience.

The buyer: Some designers work closely with buyers; others have little contact outside of a friendly "hello" in the showroom. Given a chance, buyers can contribute greatly to the designer's timing—which means showing the right design in the right fabric at the right time. A buyer sometimes receives requests from customers for a particular kind of dress; he may look for it and have trouble finding it in the market. Usually, he will then mention it to a designer pointing out, say, that his past experience leads him to expect a considerable demand next fall for color-

ful, sleeveless wool cocktail dresses. In this way, the buyer brings the designer one step closer to actual market needs.

Being a fashion buyer is a difficult job. Fall choices have to be made in May and June and spring buying in late summer and early fall and it's hard to anticipate that far in advance what customers will want. The buyer relies on his (or her) own experience to spot what's new and coming and also on tips from the fashion magazines, the trade periodicals and newspapers, on reports from Paris, on what the fabric houses, the fashion services, and the store's own fashion co-ordinator say. In addition, out-of-town buyers look to their store's New York buying office for information.

When all these sources add up to a common consensus of opinion—that, for instance, turtlenecks are in and hot pink is the coming color—the buyer's problems are eased. In any case, he usually makes a thorough survey of his market

before he places orders. There's a saying in the retail business, that saving shoe leather is the most expensive thing a buyer can do on a market trip.

There are two kinds of buyers: the department-store buyer, and the resident buyer, who works for a central buying office and selects garments for stores in several cities. The department-store buyer is, in many instances, in business for him-self. He's allotted a certain amount of floor space, a certain amount of money, and how he spends it is up to him. However, there must always be a relationship between his sales figures and his inventory and the store controller watches this closely. Many buyers work partly on commission, so a good season means extra money to them.

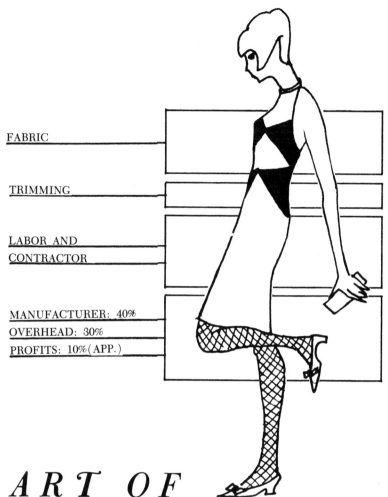

FABRIC

TRIMMING

LABOR AND
CONTRACTOR

MANUFACTURER: 40%
OVERHEAD: 30%
PROFITS: 10%(APP.)

THE ART OF JUGGLING COSTS

THE designer who knows cost handles her collection with a surer hand. She probably begins a new position by having a good, solid discussion with her employer about the price limits he feels must be set on fabric, trimming, and labor. This prevents disappointments later on. Designers for couture houses, of course, have a fairly free hand on costs, but in a medium- or lower-priced firm a balance has to be worked out. If the designer falls in love with an expensive fabric and believes it's beautiful, timely, and belongs in her collection, then she knows she must keep labor costs and trimming at a minimum to stay within her price-limit; emphasis will have to be on the fabric itself or possibly on a new silhouette. Labor detail in one area of design often necessitates simplicity in other areas. Extravagant trimming means labor costs must be cut and a less-expensive fabric used. It's necessary to think out the cost balance in advance; otherwise the designer whose sample had hand-made buttonholes from neckline to hem (which is overpricing in a $16.75 house) will be forced to sit back and mournfully watch her designs shipped out with machine-made buttonholes.

Some substitutions can be handled gracefully. Embroidery is often thinned out subtly, and pleating can be adjusted to maintain the feel of the sample. Sometimes, buttons, belts, and other trimmings are modified.

Ideally, stock shipped to the stores should duplicate the sample as closely as possible. The buyer definitely expects to receive her stock in the original sample fabric; if another fabric is substituted, the general feeling in the garment industry is that the style becomes another dress. Beyond that, stock that's a watered-down version of the sample the buyer bought at the showing leaves her dissatisfied, while a close duplication reinforces her confidence in the firm and will probably also sell better to the final judge: the consumer.

In the garment center, the pricing of a garment must take into consideration:

Labor: This includes operating, finishing, and pressing. Operating means the actual assembling of the garment by machine stitching. Finishing includes hemming, sewing on buttons, and all other handwork. Pressing, for expensive garments, is a highly skilled job. Added to the above labor costs in each case is something called "65% cost of living." This is 65% of the piece-workers (operators, finishers and pressers) original basic pay. The purpose is to raise their incomes to the level of today's cost of living without raising the basic piece-work scale. Theoretically this is flexible and adjusts to prevailing "costs of living."

Floor: Draping, examining, and cleaning all come under the heading of "floor" and a flat 60 to 70 cents is allowed to cover these costs in a firm whose garments wholesale from $29.75 to $49.75. Of course for garments that wholesale at $3.00, floor may cost 15 cents and in a couture house the floor labor costs may be $1.00. Draping is the hand-arranging that goes on before the final sewing; it might mean trying a bow skillfully—the kind that's hand-sewn afterwards. Examining is especially important; every dress shipped out is checked by an examiner to catch errors, to avoid returns from the stores. Cleaning means spot cleaning.

Cutting: It's sometimes done at the contractor, sometimes at the garment firm. It is considered part of the labor costs.

Contractor: When all the labor costs have been added up, the contractor works out 40% of the total (from 30 to 35% in lower-priced firms and charges that much for himself (his overhead and profit).

Fabric: This is the approximate price of the total yardage used in the garment.

Trimming: The price of whatever buttons, linings, interlinings, zippers, embroidery, tucking, pleating, artificial flowers, feathers, furs, etc. are used.

Manufacturer's profit: The garment manufacturer himself adds on 40% of the total of all the amounts above to cover overhead and profit. Overhead comes to about 30–35% and it includes the designer's salary and those of the rest of the staff, plus rent, maintenance, and so on. Ideally, the remaining 10% is profit.

A firm that does $2,000,000 worth of business in a year should make about $200,000 net profit. However, lower-priced firms work on a smaller profit margin. They sell in greater volume, and their designing staff expenses are lower since they do a great deal of copying. Their line is also smaller than that of a better house and the sample room may consist of only two or three sample hands. Also, they have no model expenses, since all samples are shown to buyers on the hanger. A hypothetical garment wholesaling at $35.75 would break down in price approximately in this manner:

$ 2.85	operating
.66	finishing
.95	pressing
$ 4.46	
2.90	65% cost of living
$ 7.36	
1.00	cutting
.60	floor-examining, draping, cleaning
$ 8.96	total labor costs
3.58	40% of labor paid to contractor
$12.54	total cost labor and contractor
2.50	trimming on garment
10.00	fabric
$25.04	Total costs
10.02	40% for manufacturer (30% overhead, approximately 10% profit)
$35.06	

This sample garment would sell for about $35.75 wholesale and $55.00 retail.

Pricing the sample: (approximate figures)

SAMPLE PRICE	TOTAL COSTS
$23.75	$14.25
25.75	15.75
26.75	16.05
28.75	17.25
29.75	17.85
31.75	19.75
32.75	19.65
35.75	21.45
39.75	23.85
45.75	27.45
49.75	29.85
55.75	33.45
59.75	35.85
65.75	39.45
69.75	41.85
75.75	45.45
79.75	47.85

The amount of the cutting ticket, and reorders as they come in, tell the designer how successfully her collection is selling. Below, in approximate figures, are examples of good cutting tickets, and average and great reorders.

Sample price	Cutting ticket	Reorders, average	Reorders on Ford
$10.75	200 or above	100 or above	4,000
16.75	200 ” ”	100 ” ”	4,000
29.75	200 ” ”	100 ” ”	3,000
39.75	150 ” ”	100 ” ”	3,000
49.75	125 ” ”	50–100 or above	3,000
59.75	100 ” ”	50–100 ” ”	3,000
69.75	100 ” ”	50 ” ”	3,000
75.75	100 ” ”	50 ” ”	800
79.75	100 ” ”	50 ” ”	800

Listed below are the approximate mark-up prices—that is, from wholesale to retail—used in most stores in the country. It's always interesting for the designer to know what prices her samples are selling for.

Wholesale	Retail	Wholesale	Retail
$ 8.75	$ 14.75		
13.75	22.95	35.00	55.00
14.75	25.00	39.95	59.95
16.75	29.95	45.00	75.00
18.75	35.00	49.75	79.95
22.75	39.95	59.00	95.00
29.75	49.95	69.95	115.00

CHOOSING FABRICS
FOR THE COLLECTION

Before beginning a collection, a designer may spend a week or two weeks visiting fabric firms, making selections. Fabric salesmen also come to her; the more successful she has been in the past, the more anxious they are to sell her something from their lines—hoping that the sample that emerges will turn out to be a Ford.

The designer must keep a careful balance in her collection between designs in basic fabrics and those in novelties, just as she keeps a balance between bread-and-butter numbers and high-style fashions. Basic fabrics are the simpler, more familiar ones, like woolens and crepes. They never really go out of fashion, though the emphasis shifts from year to year. For example, in some seasons textured crepes may be featured importantly, while at another time smooth silks will be more popular. Wools swing from the open-textured basketweaves to the more closely-woven ones. From summer to summer basic fabrics for streetwear have moved from silk shantung to silk linen, and, even more recently, to pure linen and slubbed silks.

Novelties are the more offbeat fabrics—brocade, matelassé, lamé, fake furs, lace, mohair, plaids, checks, and so on—and they tend to be quite definitely either in fashion or out of it. Shown at the right time, a novelty fabric can look very fresh and new; however, the designer who goes on a novelty binge may find the buyers crying out for staples, and her manufacturer just crying. On the other hand, there are times when a novelty that's new and hot becomes a Ford.

Fabric houses try to show what's new and currently important. They are influenced by the fabrics supplied to the Paris couture by European fabric firms, which are traditionally fashion leaders, or they may follow a trend started by an American couture designer.

Textile firms specialize, just as garment firms do. Besides the basic wool houses and cotton houses, there are firms that offer only knits, or only novelties such as brocades and metallics.

Some carry solid-color crepes in the fall and a line of beautiful prints for the resort, spring, and summer collections. There are firms that are known for velvets and velveteens, and others with a reputation for dressier fabrics—chiffons, taffetas, peau de soie, peau d'ange and silk failles. Some European textile makers have sales representatives in New York who take orders to be filled in Europe. The experienced designer is familiar with all the fabric sources; a novice designer can usually rely on her piece-goods man for guidance until she becomes familiar with the market.

A well-established textile firm usually tries for a line that's varied and, hopefully, has something for every price range, because many dress firms like to confine some fabrics. Confining is done when a fabric is unusual and new-looking; it prevents a competing dress manufacturer from offering styles in the same distinctive fabric, and it especially prevents a lower-priced house from buying it and underselling.

The giants of the garment industry usually buy their fabrics from the giants of the textile industry, since these are the firms that are geared to supply in quantity. Garment makers who are not yet securely established turn to smaller fabric firms, because they're more willing to take a chance.

Any hot fabric is soon "knocked off" by other fabric firms, large and small. After mohair became high fashion and began selling strongly in Seventh Avenue showrooms, it was copied right down the line at all price levels, turning up in coats that sold for hundreds of dollars and dresses that sold for twenty. Almost all hot novelty fabrics eventually become obsolete as fashion turns to something new.

The designer has to know what each fabric will do in relation to its end-use. For example, a recent vinyl patterned to look like alligator is obviously perfect for raincoats since it is waterproof and easy to sponge clean, while a fabric

that's lightweight, wrinkle-resistant, and that also drips dry is a natural for resort and travel clothes.

In considering a fabric for use in her collection, the designer must ask herself:

1. Is this fabric suited to the current fashion trend? As she drapes, she attempts to interpret the fabric. If the current look is molded, with architectural shape, she needs fabrics that are crisp and have body. If the trend is toward soft, drapy styles, she looks for knits, jerseys, chiffons, soft crepes and wools. However, the effect of the fabric can be changed by the kind of backing, lining and interlining that are used. These run the gamut from some that are so soft they merely give a little body to the garment, to firmer ones that give mold and shape. Knowing what a fabric can do—and what it can be made to do when it's lined—is part of the designer's basic knowhow, and it's as much a creative skill as it is a technical one.

2. The designer also asks herself about the practical performance of the fabric: Will it shrink? Will it fade or run? Shrinkage can be tested easily by measuring. Fading and color-running are checked by a simple, table-top-test—the fabric is rubbed hard to see if it crocks off. Textile manufacturers are supposed to check performance themselves and reputable houses are usually reliable, but because returns have a very bad effect on a garment firm nothing should be taken for granted.

Left: Rudi Gernreich selecting a fabric.

Ann Klein:
Experimenting with fabric.

CREATING

IN FABRICS

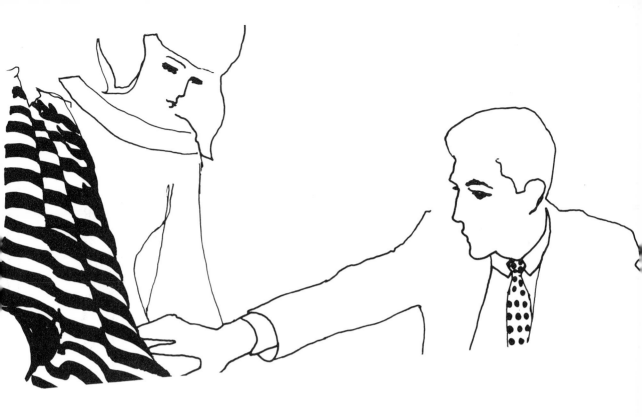

Fabric is the designer's creative medium, just as pigment is the painter's. A good designer responds to new fabrics and attempts to catch it's mood in a new way. She fingers the cloth, drapes it on a model, searches for the quality that will make it—and her design—come alive. Sometimes a fabric seems created for a design of a particular kind. Then, again, some of the freshest-looking fashions over the years have used familiar fabrics in unexpected ways. Chanel, in her Fall 1964 collection, lined colorful wool tweed suits with glittery lamé; Pucci made fashion history with his brilliantly printed silk jerseys which fold up so small that a woman can pack a collection of them in a canvas airline bag and jet around the world.

Some of the fabrics designers work with are thousands of years old; others emerged from the test tube just yesterday. Silk is said to have been first discovered by Hsi-ling-shi, the fourteen-year-old bride of a Chinese emperor, about 2640 B.C. The emperor's mulberry grove was being de-stroyed by tiny white worms that banqueted on its leaves and decorated the trees with neat white cocoons. Hsi-ling-shi collected a handful of cocoons and brought them to her rooms. There, she accidentally dropped one into a basin of hot water. Playing with it in the water, she unwound a delicate, seemingly endless white thread. The Chinese kept the secret of the silk cocoon for nearly 3,000 years. Camel caravans carried woven Chinese silks across Asia to Damascus, where they were traded for Western luxuries. Silks from China were unravelled in Persia and re-woven into Persian designs for wear at court, and for a time Persia controlled the silk that came out of China, reselling it in the West at fantastic prices. In 550 A.D. the Byzantine Emperor, Justinian, seeking to break the Persian monopoly, sent two monks to China, where they stole mulberry seeds and silk worm eggs, hid them in their walking staffs, and brought them back to Byzantium. After that, silk culture moved across Europe, often in the wake of a conquering nation.

[79]

XVII Century Indian printed fabric hanging.

Wool is even older than silk. It was around 6,000 B.C. that man realized that one animal, the sheep, could provide many of his basic needs: food, clothing that was softer and warmer than the hairy skins of other animals, and tents to shelter him when he traveled. Sheep, he learned, were also gregarious and easy to herd; in domesticating the sheep, he became more civilized himself. By 4,000 B.C. sheepskins were being replaced in some parts of the world by woven wool garments and by 2,500 B.C. wool-growing was a major industry in Mesopotamia. The development of wool from the first raw fleece coverings to the luxurious fabrics of today kept pace with man's

long progress from the cave to the sky-scraper.

At the beginning of this century in Europe, there were three primary fabrics and their uses were rigidly defined. Silk, which came mainly from France, was considered a dressy, evening fabric and was worn mostly by the upper classes. Wool, which came from England, was for morning wear and it was the fabric also of the middle classes. Cotton was strictly for the poor. It wasn't until the 1920's that Chanel made wool fashionable for formal wear and also used it instead of silk in suits; she experimented with cotton, too, but it wasn't considered acceptable in evening clothes until Balenciaga, in 1936, used piqué and striped cottons for a series of long dresses.

The first of the man-made fabrics was "art silk", a harsh, sleazy-looking rayon that was developed in the nineteenth century. Between the World Wars it was improved and its name was changed to rayon, but it really came into its own when the scarcities caused by World War II forced it to the public's attention. After the war, top designers began to work enthusiastically with synthetics. Dozens of new ones were developed and dozens of confusing new polysyllabic nouns were added to the language.

Today, fabrics are available in more variety and with more texture interest than ever before, and there are more unusual-looking fabrics to choose from. The development of new fabrics has made new kinds of fashion possible. Dresses can be shaped with real crispness, or they can have a wonderful softness when they're made with light, fluffy fabrics. Since the advent of permanent-pleating, pleats have become quite practical. For a while the new synthetics were widely advertised as "miracle fabrics." Because they sometimes didn't live up to their advance billing, the public soon became wary. Over the years, though, synthetics have been worked on and improved, and advertisers have learned not to promise too much.

By and large, and in varying degrees, fabrics have been developed that are stronger and longer-wearing than earlier synthetics; are easier to wash and quicker to dry; require little or no ironing, are much more wrinkle-resistant than before; and are moth- and mildew-proof.

Immersing cocoons for easy reeling, 4,600 year old process.

Slip has black stretch bra. Printed nylon tricot chemise.

FABRICS OF THE FUTURE

Never before in the 8,000 year of textiles has there been so much excitement in the fabric field—nor has the fashion designer been so aware of fibers and so knowledgeable about their performance. The impact today of a blossoming technology bears comparison with the great period of textile invention of the eighteenth century. Spurred on by earlier discoveries in man-made fabrics, this period has achieved a series of breakthroughs that began with the newer synthetics and their blends, swiftly followed by Wash-Wear, Stretch, Permanent Press and Fabric-to-Fabric Bonding. Non-wovens like paper and plastic are also making an interesting dent in the fashion picture.

Synthetics and blends—As large companies spur more and more research, fashion designers will be constantly challenged by future developments. Synthetics are being used more and more in *blends,* with other man-made fabrics and with natural fibers—to achieve fuller creativity and service. Paris Couturiers have welcomed blends for some time. In 1957 Lanvin launched a mixture of nylon and mohair in a group of coats that were wonderfully lightweight without sag. The Italian designer, Pucci, promoted a jersey that was a blend of cashmere, nylon and wool—soft, luxurious, and it traveled beautifully. What's tricky about blends is the percentage of each fiber used. Testing goes on constantly to find out what proportions work best for particular uses. Sometimes to get the maximum of one quality, such as abrasion-resistance, another must be sacrificed; however if it's not important to the fabric's end use, it won't be missed.

Stretch—One of the most important recent developments has been the advent of stretch fabrics. They got their start in sportswear with ski pants mainly and are moving swiftly into children's wear, dresses, men's wear and other

Stella Brooks designs a wine plastic dress with yellow frieze at hem for Paraphenalia.

[85]

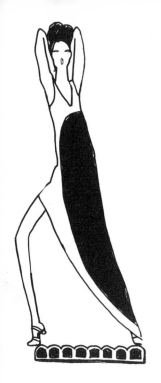

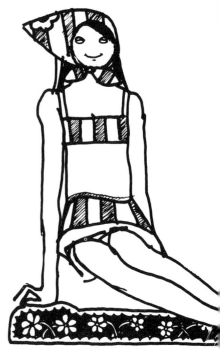

Paper . . . for resort, '67.

apparel areas. Some observers predict, by the end of the decade, 90% of all apparel will have some stretch properties. There are several different methods of making stretchy materials. One of the first was to coil-crimp the yarn: it was twisted, set with heat, then untwisted—and it behaved like a coil spring. A newer method uses a center core of elastic fiber wrapped with yarn. The early enthusiasm for stretch resulted in some unsatisfactory fabrics and gave stretch, temporarily, a bad reputation, but it is already on the way to overcoming this. The discovery of stretch will have many effects. Clothes can now be shaped closer to the body with more freedom of movement and less alteration. Because stretch fabrics are resilient, baggy knees on trousers should almost disappear; today's children's clothes stretch to accommodate growing young bodies. Slips and nightgowns are now being produced with stretch tops that double as brassieres. Stretch imparts unusual wrinkle-shedding properties.

Permanent Press (Durable Press)—It has been said that durable press—sometimes called permanent press—is a major landmark in the textile industry, one that will rank in importance with the advent of man-made fibers. Within a few short years billions of yards of fabric have been treated with this new technique. Durable press is the ultimate in wash and wear. There are two types of durable press, pre-cured and post-cured. Pre-cured refers to fabrics that have been treated with special resin finishes prior to their being cut and sewn into a garment. The manufacturer can complete the garment, then pleats can be put in and wrinkles removed by pressing with special hot-head presses within controlled temperature and pressure limits. Post-cured fabrics are treated with special resins, then made into a garment. The final step requires oven treatment of the finished garment to lock in the durable press features.

Fabric-to-Fabric-Bonding — Bonded fabrics were launched in 1962. By 1970 it is predicted that more than 400 million yards of acetate tricot alone will be used as lining fabric. A bonded textile is one in which a face fabric has been

fused to a lining fabric, and in nine cases out of ten, the liner is an acetate or nylon tricot. Basic to the process was the development of new adhesives—chiefly the acrylics and the urethanes—which made it possible to achieve a permanent bond between two fabrics, without destroying the soft hand or drape of the cloth; a bond which would survive washing and dry cleaning. The new techniques have made it possible to take an unstable textile structure and give it stability. This means that lace constructions as well as very loose open weaves can be manufactured into designs that were at one time unworkable. The science of bonding or laminating one fabric permanently to another has opened new concepts in tailoring of knits, giving them stability necessary for the cutting table and drape for the fashion creator. More economical in production, it makes possible the single cutting of two fabrics simultaneously. For the fashion designer the virtue of bonding (also called double-face fabric when another technique for adhering two fabrics is used) is that it provides infinite pos-

sibilities for combining different fabrics of varied construction, color combinations and texture. It extends the performance, appearance and end use of fabric many times over. The future holds further aesthetic possibilities inherent in the new technique yet to be explored.

Paper—A flood of publicity from jubilant fashion writers in 1966 and early 1967 seemed to underline the interest by the apparel industry in clothes made of paper. A premium offer of a paper dress for one dollar by the Scott Paper Company in 1965 started the ball rolling—in no time high fashion and boutique designers, with much hoopla, were testing their talents in paper. A much publicized "paper dress party" with imaginative and clever designs led to a new topic of conversation, and to a definite test of paper clothes by many customers. By early 1967 about six manufacturers were making paper garments. Estimates in the industry in this period were that about 1.4 million garments made of paper or paper-like fabric were sold since the beginning of 1966. The total retail value of

Jantzen's silver and gold bikinis with vinyl cover-ups, Resort, '67.

paper clothing in 1966 was about $3.5 million out of an estimated $30 billion spent by the nation's female consumers for apparel.

Some non-woven fabrics are "Kaycel", a cellulose wadding reinforced by a nylon scrim, consisting of 93% cellulose and 3% nylon and "Dura-weve" made of several layers of a napkin base reinforced by a rayon scrim laminated into the layers—another company is making an all rayon disposable fabric. In the future are more non-woven materials, now in the experimental stage, with a molecular make-up like that of paper or plastic.

Some top retail executives feel that the paper dress is basically a fun thing, a fad, and on a long range basis see it more important in the industrial and utility field—other top retailers and buyers feel most enthusiastic. However, paper garments, ranging from sportswear to bras and children's wear (with an abundance of good fashion design) are being produced by some noted manufacturers. It has been said that paper apparel's biggest contribution may turn out to be the fact that it has stirred the imagination of many designers, manufacturers and sellers of apparel making them aware of not only the possibilities of disposable garments, but also the entire realm of technological possibilities in todays' mode of living.

Plastic-Vinyl—The plastic-vinyl materials are swinging in with the "Youth Movement" which has engulfed the Paris Couturiers and apparently the rest of the fashion world. One of the original innovators is Pasco Rabanne, the French designer, who created a stir when he designed whole dresses of loose hanging glittering circles of plastic that looked like giant paillettes. In a recent boutique collection he used a transparent phosphorescent rhodoid plastic—and designed plastic dresses with hoops and resembling onion rings. Chanel in her Spring '67 collection used vinyl— it made the black scarf and cuffs on the fuschia suit jacket of number 5—always Chanel's favorite in a collection. In New York, a price tag on a raincoat that Oscar de la Renta designed for Jane Derby recently was $395. In clear plastic, studded with rhinestones that looked something like raindrops, it took on different hues with everything that was worn under it. Pauline Trigère used see-through vinyl alternating with bands of fabric for an evening dress in her recent summer collection—and wide clear vinyl belts. Boutique designers have been showing dresses in colored plastic that look like leather and Tiffeau's models in his recent summer collection dangled Lucite jewelry and wore clear plastic shoes.

From the designer's point of view, fabrics, both woven and non-woven, have never offered more of a challenge and the future looks very bright. Fabrics today have properties that we never dreamed were possible, and it seems certain that in years to come new abilities and new color effects that are unimaginable, even now, will develop. The design possibilities are tremendously exciting.

A summary of current man-made fibers:

GENERIC NAME (*listed are some of best-known*)	TRADE NAME	ADVANTAGES AND OTHER QUALITIES
nylon	(varied)	Abrasion resistance, excellent strength and wearing quality, quick drying.
acrylic fibers	Orlon, Acrilan, Creslan, Zefran	Easy to dye, good bulk, warmth, wool-like texture
polyester fibers	Kodel, Fortrel, Dacron, Vycron	Great resilience, stretch resistance, ease in washing, ironing and damp creasing, easily blended with other fabrics. Used for Durable Press in blends with cotton.
spandex	Lycra, Vyrene	Elastic fiber used for swim wear, girdles, bras, increasingly used for stretch fabrics.
acetate	Avisco, Estron Acele	Low fiber cost, porous and cool, not terribly strong, good draping qualities, high sheen, wears poorly, high fashion at low price.
triacetate	Arnel	Crease-resistant, new form of acetate, better wash and wear than regular acetate, permanently pleated.
rayon	(varied)	Early man-made fiber, many properties of cotton but much weaker, some types have high sheen.
high modulus cotton	(varied)	Can be laundered and handled like cotton; smoother and silkier in appearance, looks like fine-combed better cotton when blended with cheaper cotton.
modacrylic	Dynel	Very useful in pile fabrics, gaining popularity for hairpieces.

Directoire (1795–1804).

THE DESIGNER'S
SEARCH
FOR INSPIRATION

Fashions in hair (1788).

FASHION is change: the new becoming old and old ideas becoming new again—but always with a fresh twist (art historians call it "putting old wine in new bottles"). The continual search for something fresh is the designer's greatest challenge. Buyers, arriving on Seventh Avenue, hope to see something so new-looking it will make yesterday's clothes seem outdated. The designer's greatest challenge is the ever-recurring dilemma: "How can I make my next collection look new?"

In her pursuit of the new, she draws from many sources. She watches for the earliest hints of coming trends, she may review fashions of the past, she turns to the entertainment world and to international fashion leaders for ideas; technological developments and world events also influence her thinking.

Current Trends: For many designers, reading *Women's Wear Daily* is a morning ritual, and one good way to keep up with what's happening in fashion. *Vogue, Harper's Bazaar, L'Officiel,* and other fashion magazines are also followed closely.

Some designers make a ritual of a weekly tour of Fifth Avenue. Here, they can linger over store windows that display a St. Laurent original, or one by Norell. Just as artists visit museums and galleries to see and be stimulated by the work of other artists, so designers learn from the work of their contemporaries. New York windows show cleverly thought-out new cuts and shapes, new tricks in construction, new trends, from all over the world. In fine weather, a walk on Fifth Avenue might also net the designer a glimpse of a Dior suit stepping out of a taxi, or a Galanos dress emerging from a revolving door. She returns to her designing room and

Poiret, Paris 1913.

*Costume designs
for Scheherazade
(1910).*

her work feeling refreshed, and possibly she brings back a few ideas to experiment with.

Most designers watch the Paris openings closely. There has always been a great deal of controversy over whether American designers should follow the lead of the Paris couture houses, or create on their own. The question, we think is academic; it's like asking whether American artists at the turn of the century should have ignored the French Impressionists. Great art inspires no matter where it is produced, and nothing is gained by denying its influence. Paris, is, in its turn, influenced by American mass production techniques. The new trend for the Paris couturier is the design of ready-to-wear, to supply their own boutiques for the young well-to-do clients who are too busy to go through interminable fittings. This is in addition to their regular collections. French couturiers in the past designed mainly for the highly-sophisticated mature woman, while in the United States the emphasis was on youth; in recent years Paris fashions have been looking younger and younger. The 1967 enthusiasm for pants, boutique and controversial clothing was anticipated long ago in the United States and England. Fashion is becoming, more and more, a world-wide exchange of ideas, with trends often started simultaneously in several countries.

Paris provides the ideal environment for the designer. Since French couturiers are not creating for a mass market, they can afford to be experimental. Clients are wealthy and affluent, therefore collections can be sumptuous and expensive, using richly designed fabric and elegant ornamentation. And the artisans of France provide the best as they have for centuries. Quality is the tradition; French fabrics and accessories are

*Norell
adaptation
(1964).*

the most luxurious, the most beautiful, in the world. The Paris couture has unique stature—for centuries, since the time of Marie Antoinette, the city has been the world's fashion center—and, in addition, in Paris there's a special interplay between the arts. Dior was once an art dealer; Chanel was a friend of Cocteau's; Dufy and Bakst did textile designs. When Courrèges was recently asked about the influence of art on fashion, Mr. Courrèges said that "the most rigorous works of Kandinsky had inspired him," but he added that one factor in the "logical composition" of his clothes had been his careful study of the "great architects" of today, above all others Le Corbusier and Saarinen.

With the temporary eclipse of the French couture during World War II, designers in other countries gained in prestige. Today, the world follows not only the French collections, but also the Italian and Spanish ones, and the major American openings—those of Norell, Bill Blass,

*American
Cloak and Suit
Review 1914.*

Rudi Gernreich, Donald Brooks, Trigère and Galanos. The woman who owns a Dior dress is apt to own a Norell and a Galanos, too. However, the crucial event of the year for the fashion world is still the Paris openings, and the definitive changes still originate, most of the time, in France.

The Entertainment World: The designer mines ideas from the theater, from films, ballet, and opera. Period movies and films whose stars are noted for high fashion are especially good sources, as are old films. One designer recently confessed that he spends frequent sleepless nights watching the late, late movies on television to get the feel of the fashions of the thirties.

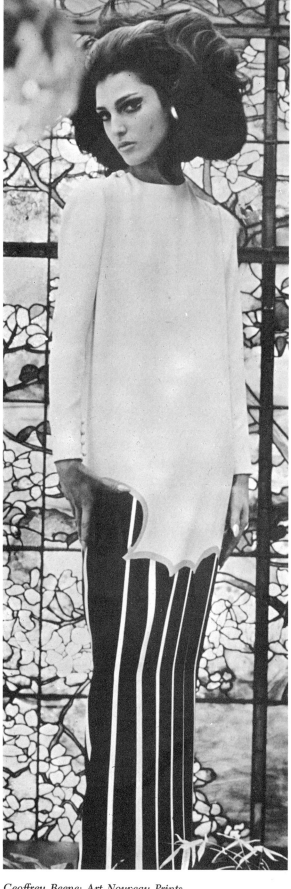

Geoffrey Beene: Art Nouveau Prints.

The entertainment world has always had an influence on fashion. In 1910 Diaghilev's Russian Ballet was the talk of Paris and its performance of Scheherazade set off a wave of Orientalism. Describing it, a contemporary writer said:

"Almost immediately could be perceived the influence which the debauch of violent colors was to exercise on painting, costumes, and interior decoration. Fundamentally, it was yet once more the thousand-color Orient bursting into our grey and monotonous life and overflowing it."

A Paris designer named Paul Poiret had become intrigued by the Orient at about the same time. His collections, and others of the period, began the tradition of the great Paris openings. For the first time, socialites flocked to the couture houses as they would have to the theater, expecting to see beautiful models in a luxurious setting —and something startlingly new in fashion. Poiret gave them all this and more; he also organized society parties, the most famous his Thousand and Second Night in 1911. Guests attended in Persian costumes and Poiret's house was filled with blue and gold Persian tents.

Started by Poiret and the Russian Ballet, the interest in Orientalism boomed. Harem skirts, worn by a few bold spirits, were chased off the streets—just as women had been chased from the street years before, in 1795, for appearing in the directoire fashions that bared the breasts. But harem skirts led to hobble skirts, which had the same silhouette, and these were finally adopted enthusiastically by almost everyone. This was a stunning change from the shapes of preceding years—from the time when women were, as the famous actress, Mrs. Patrick Campbell, put it, "all bosoms and bottoms." The new silhouette lasted for about five years, from 1909 until the First World War began in late 1914.

In recent times, the entertainment world's influence has been maintained mainly through the medium of films. The movie *Tom Jones,* led to Tom Jones shirts and Tom Jones hairdos. The

*Larry Aldrich
with Op Art painting
from his collection.*

*Op Art adaptation
by designer
for Larry Aldrich.*

Influenced by travel are St. Laurent's Rajah Coat (left) and Balenciaga's Sari Gown (1964).

battle scenes in the film, *Dr. Zhivago*, were the inspiration for the long military coats, shown with high boots and a rash of military épaulettes, in the Paris '66 Fall collections.

Fashion Leaders: Throughout history there have been women who set the fashion for their own day. Usually, they had great beauty and a strong fashion sense as well as a position of importance in society. In modern America, actresses, society women, and other women in public life are the style-setters. Jacqueline Kennedy's look in particular—her simple, sleeveless skimmy dresses—made their mark. Designers watch the newspapers to see what's being worn at the White House and at important society events.

The Queens and Empresses of France and the Queens of England were often trend-setters, but Marie Antoinette is perhaps the classic example. She spent so lavishly for clothes and fabulous jewelry that she had to take up gambling to pay her debts. It is said that each morning a servant would appear in her chambers carrying a huge book filled with drawings of all her clothes; from this she would select her costume for the day. Upkeep on her wardrobe required a small army of maids and seamstresses. The ladies of the court vied to imitate her, sometimes contrived to bribe her dressmaker for a copy of a dress the Queen had not yet had time to wear.

The dressmaker, Mademoiselle Bertin, was the

Marlene Dietrich, 1933.

first really famous couturier. Before her time dolls were used as models, dressed up so that clients could select a costume. In colonial times the dolls were sometimes sent out from Paris and women in America would also choose from the "collection." Bertin was the first to make full-size models of her designs. She was of common birth, rude and opinionated, but she had more power at the court than any ministers of state.

The Queen's hairdresser, Monsieur Leonard, was another power. Every morning he drove out from Paris to Versailles in a handsome six-in-hand to do Marie Antoinette's hair. Using huge hairpins and stiff pomade, he constructed towering edifices of hair, and at the top, eighteen full inches above eyebrow-level, he created tiny tableaux: fruit gardens, ships at sea in a storm. Great events of the day were reconstructed on the coiffure top: a scene from a new opera, the king's smallpox vaccination, the American Revolution. And, of course, the ladies of the court were quick to copy the Queen's hair styles. Coifs grew higher and higher, until the doorways at the Versailles had to be made taller and taller, and ladies could no longer sit in their carriages, but were forced to kneel on the floor. While the first stirrings of the French Revolution filled the air around them, they talked only of the newest hairdos, and of Mademoiselle Bertin's latest designs.

World Events: Fashion has always mirrored the world it exists in—the values and dreams of its era. The exaggerated styles of Marie Antoinette's day reflected the decadence of court life; after the French Revolution, the fashion changed radically. The new Directoire look harked back to ancient Greece and Rome, whose democratic life was now much admired. Women wore simple, diaphanous garments with Empire waists and low necklines, and sandals often laced up high on the leg. It was a period of exhilarating emancipation, a time of dancing and a certain fine recklessness, and its spirit was kin to that of the 1920's. Women tossed away the tight stomachers and stiff corseting that had bound them for so long, and cut their hair short. The daring went out in bare-breasted dresses—and were promptly chased from the streets. It was a time, too, that had its own grisly sense of humor; for a while at the highly fashionable balls it was the fashion for women to wear a red ribbon about their throats—a reminder of the guillotine—and to greet acquaintances with a sharp twitch of the neck as if the head were about to topple off.

Directoire fashions gave way to a romantic period, and then, in Queen Victoria's day, prudery put women back into tight corsets and high necklines. The only parts of the body that showed were face, hands, and the tips of the toes.

With the outbreak of the First World War, there was a second emancipation. Before the war, most women's lives were lived out within their own home; it was the rare women who worked, drove a car, or participated in sports. When the war came, filling in for men in factories and offices, and liking their new life, they demanded new freedoms—including freedom in dress. In the Twenties, corsets were discarded (again); skirts got shorter and so did hair. Apparently equating freedom with masculinity, women adopted a boyish look—flat-chested, straight up and down. Chanel, responding to the *zeitgeist,* the spirit of the times, introduced the chemise—first one or two, then perhaps half a dozen, until suddenly everyone else began making them, too. It was not just a case of one designer decreeing a new style, but rather of a designer of great talent sensing the mood of the times and the look that it demanded.

In the Thirties there was a reaction against the flapper styles, and a super-feminine look came into being. Small tri-corn hats often with curling ostrich feathers (Empress Eugenie inspired), tight little jackets, flowing jabots and ruching were part of it.

During the Second World War women replaced

Amelia Bloomer (1818–1894).

*Paris,
pants
1967.*

men in the factories and offices again, and fashion once more took a turn for the more masculine. There were broad, padded shoulders, there was new acceptance for slacks, and a military look was often evident. Because of the shortage of fabrics, three and a half yards was the most that was allowed for a sample garment; skirts therefore, were short and skimpy.

After the war's end, a new Paris designer, Dior, responding as Chanel had to the *zeitgeist,* created the New Look. With his first post-war collection, he launched a return to femininity, a joyous revolution after the restrictions of the war. Waists were tiny, hips padded; hemlines dropped dramatically and skirts were full; shoulders took on a gently sloping Victorian look. To get the tiny waistlines the new fashions demanded, the more fashionable women all over the world bound themselves with cinchers—wide elasticized bands that clamped in the waist, rounded the hips.

Today, sensitive designers respond to the same factors in modern life that influence architects, artists, musicians, and writers. Fashions have become very simple, very streamlined, as have buildings, while art, music, and writing have tended toward the abstract. As lines became simpler in fashion, texture has assumed new importance (hence the popularity of chiffon, leather and grainy woolens) and color has grown more vivid. Clothes seen on Fifth Avenue today make clothes from any period before the last war look drab. Designers have responded, too, to the modern move to suburbia and its informal, active way of life. Beautifully cut pants have arrived and become increasingly important, as have culottes and shorts.

Throughout the history of mankind, probably more women than men wore trousers. Oriental civilizations with their high ethical standards often completely reversed the clothing of the sexes. Their robed men were never thought of as effeminate or their trouser-clad women as masculine. The early Greeks did without distinct clothes

for the sexes; so did the Asiatic races like the Persians and Assyrians. The Hungarians, Greeks and Scots are examples, in later costume history, of men who liked to don more or less voluminous skirts. In America what Amelia Bloomer had on her mind in 1851 was "the evils of drink," but it is what she wore on her legs that gave her a place in history. The so-called "Turkish Costume" which carries her name was one of the earliest forms of pants worn by women in this country. They were a thoroughly modest pair of trousers gathered at the ankle and worn under a shortened skirt. Originally adopted for outdoor work by women of the Oneida community in 1848—a Mrs. Miller tried it out and Mrs. Bloomer and a friend quickly made copies for themselves. Horace Greeley's *Tribune* spread their notoriety around the country and the trousers were immediately christened "bloomers." It was useless for Amelia to protest that it was Mrs. Miller who first wore them, her name was infinitely funnier. She toured the country lecturing on temperence and suffrage in them, but finally had to cast them aside because of the ridicule. But as women became more emancipated, new generations of females (for active sports) happily wore pants, shorts and eventually bikinis. In 1966 pants came into their own in every area of dress. It was the year the fashion for wearing elegant pajamas went steadily ahead. Pajamas in highly fashionable circles became a must as an alternative for dinner dresses. The smoking suit was a hit, and the honest-to-goodness pants suit was designed from budget to Couture. In 1967 with hemlines still ascending, Paris, New York and California couture designers rediscovered shorts and designed them in every conceivable manner, under short dresses (sometimes as "bloomers"), mini shorts with jackets or under evening dresses with highly-slashed side seams.

Designers who can, often travel to find ideas, may adapt the fashions of other countries. St. Laurent glamorized the rajah coat; and Grès and Balenciaga based evening collections on

Dior's "New Look"
(post-World War II).

The "Wisp" — tiny wasp-waist belt which swept the Paris openings. Little boned miracle, it subtracts up to two inches from the middle for wear under new reed - waisted gowns—is even the darling of Paris's slim mannequins. Macy's adaptation in grosgrain and boning, 7.04. Corset Salon, Second Floor No mail, phone orders.

R. H. Macy's advertises the wasp-waist belt to wear under the Dior "New Look", 1946.

the East Indian sari. More recently an African journey inspired St. Laurent, while a vicarious trip by way of an African Art exhibit in Paris stimulated Marc Bohan of Dior. The Dior "African look" was a series of Safari suits, and for evening, bare-shouldered jungle prints. St. Laurent's trip into Africa produced bared midriffs under long chains of wooden or glass beads, Ubangi collars and yard-high African hairdos over fine wire. In New York the collection of Molly Parnis reflected her recent African safari.

Travel has long been a rich source of ideas. When Admiral Perry opened up Japan in 1854, the Western world was delighted with its discovery of Japanese art; this had an enormous influence on interior decoration, modern painting, books, opera, and fashion. Today, even the *way* people travel has its influence; jet flights have created a demand for lightweight, packable clothes—lightly lined and resistant to wrinkles; jet travel has also encouraged the boom in wash-and-wear.

New York: Manhattan itself can be a rich source of ideas for the alert designer. Faced with a "dry" period—a time when ideas just don't seem to emerge—she may decide to treat herself to an afternoon at one of the city's museums. If the paintings don't lift her creative spirits, there are always the costume sections at the Metropolitan and at the Brooklyn Museum. A few hours spent browsing through antique shops, an evening at the theatre, the opera, or a movie—all these can pay off in inspiration.

Designers say that there's something in the very atmosphere of New York that's stimulating. It has most of the great fashion schools, of course, and the leading fashion magazines are published here. But more than that, it's the whole, fascinating atmosphere. Manhattan is the creative center of the country and it attracts the most talented from all the states and from abroad as well; to a designer with her eyes open, it can't help but be an excellent source of ideas and inspiration.

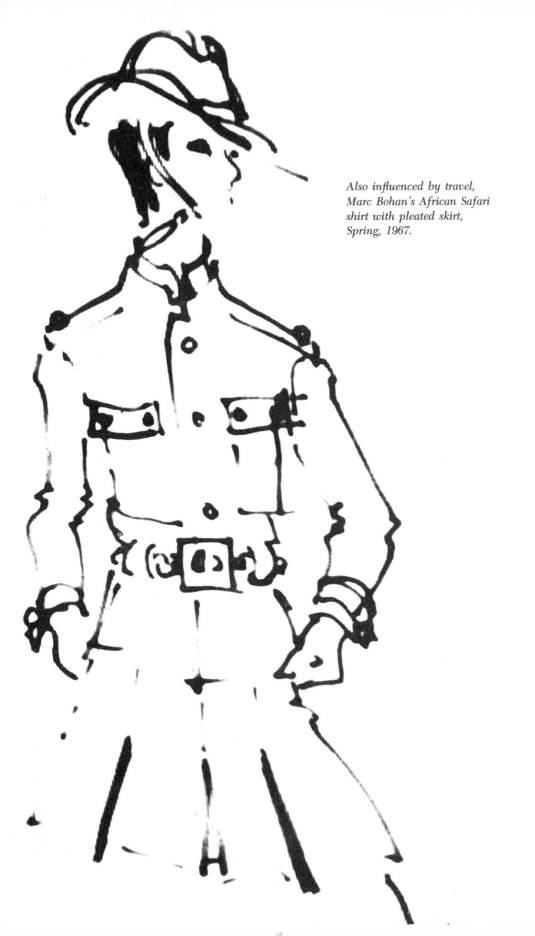

Also influenced by travel,
Marc Bohan's African Safari
shirt with pleated skirt,
Spring, 1967.

Broadway Scene (1905).

THE PAST

As FAR BACK as 1840, New York was the fashion center of the country and Broadway the great promenade. At the fashionable hour, from two to three, the roadway streamed with hackney coaches, cabs, phaetons, and handcarts, with handsomely dressed women and young men; on the fringes of the crowd there were the barefoot girls who swept the crossing, the ragged boys hawking matches and newspapers.

"Heaven save the ladies," wrote a contemporary observer of the scene. "How they dress! We have seen more colors in these ten minutes than we should have seen elsewhere in as many days. What various parasols, what rainbow silks and satins, what pinching of thin shoes, and fluttering of ribbons and silk tassels, and display of rich cloaks with gaudy hoods and linings."

In those days, of course, fashion was strictly for the rich. The "rainbow silks and satins" were hand-sewn by tailors and dressmakers, or were imported from Europe. The poor sewed their own garments at home—and it was the poor who supplied the incentive for a ready-to-wear industry, which didn't come into being in America until roughly a hundred years ago.

At first, only seamen and slaves wore ready-made clothes; Brooks Brothers got its start in Bedford, Massachusetts, about 1830, making

Early Skirt Factory (1859).

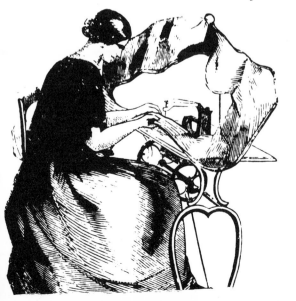

clothes for sailors. But as the population grew, secondhand dealers found they could no longer supply the demand for ready-to-wear and so they began to have clothes made.

The early garment workers were farm women, sewing at home on fabrics supplied to them. Gradually, some began to work in groups. The invention of the sewing machine was all that was needed, now, to prepare the way for real factories, and Elias Howe produced such a machine in 1846. There'd been an earlier one invented by a man named Barthelemy Themmonier in 1829 in Paris; however, during the disturbances of 1830, when barricades went up in the streets, his machines were destroyed by the mob and he was driven from the city for fear his invention would cause unemployment.

By 1860 there was ready-to-wear for women; retailers and wholesalers in the larger cities had begun having hoop skirts and cloaks manufactured and factories developed in the cities to supply them. The American Civil War, with its demands for army uniforms, further spurred the infant industry.

The garment labor force in those early days was made up mostly of Irish and German immigrants and it was 88% female. New York City, as a ready source of cheap immigrant labor, was a natural center for the industry. It had that other attraction, too: it was already a fashion center, pace-setter for the rest of the country.

The industry developed slowly. At the turn of the century women were still leading home-bound, Victorian lives. Most ladies of moderate means owned three dresses, a "best" dress, an everyday one, and a house dress, with shirtwaists and skirts to fill in. The shirtwaists and skirts were among the first garments to be mass produced; dresses were too elaborate, decked as they were with ruffles and flounces, their fit calculated to a hair-breadth to emphasize hourglass figures. This made them unsuitable for mass production methods, and alterations would have been too costly, anyway. However, with the First World War, the emancipation of women, and the dramatic changes in fashion, ready-to-wear came into its own. In 1918 the first single-piece tubular dress was shown and it was an instant suc-

The Sweat Shop (1905).

Piece Work, turn of the century.

cess; it was very simple, easy to make in a factory.

In the Twenties Americans were more prosperous than ever before and had more leisure time, so fashion became more important to them. The flapper era had varying effects on the garment industry. Corsets were replaced by panty girdles—they were all woman needed if she had a boyish figure and wore her stockings rolled. The shoe industry thrived after the advent of short skirts, and the sportswear industry came into being as women escaped from home-bound routines. On the other hand, hat-frame firms were dealt a stunning blow when cropped hair came into fashion, making elaborate hat-sizing unnecessary.

At first almost all ready-to-wear was moderately priced and quite conservative. Most styles were adaptations or copies of Paris fashions; however, because the American way of life was not identical with the French way, manufacturers were forced to employ more and more designers to make necessary changes in styles. During the First World War, no French imports reached the

United States and the American fashion industry benefited. Despite this, after the war, they still had very little prestige. Various American organizations tried to help by publicizing the industry's achievements and the names of the most talented designers—most of whom still worked anonymously. In 1914 *Vogue* magazine sponsored a Fashion Fête to encourage American design, and in 1916 *Women's Wear Daily* held the first of five annual contests for textile designers. But the Paris Exposition of Decorative Arts in 1925 came as a rude shock; no American designs were included because the French authorities claimed there was nothing worthwhile enough to include. American designers defended themselves, saying manufacturers and the public insisted on copies of European designs and wouldn't accept anything original. Museums took up the cause and gave exhibitions of the best in American design, eventually proving there was a market for it after all.

The 1920's brought the first of the big-name garment firms and the first famous U.S. designers; it was the beginning of the industry as we know it today. Some of the earliest names were those of Hattie Carnegie, William Bloom, and Peggy Hoyt. Finally, with World War II, the French fashion houses were once again eclipsed, with huge new gains for American designers.

Courrèges and line-for-line copy.

THE PRESENT

A young American designing in Thailand.

THE garment industry today operates in true free-enterprise style; it's still a 19th century phenomenon in many ways. There are thousands of small manufacturers (12,000 in the tiny Manhattan garment center alone) and most firms are personally owned and run. Competition is keen and success doesn't depend on new equipment or the latest production techniques, but on the talent and business sense of the key members of each firm. As in the 19th century, there are enormous profits to be made, but there are also risks: every year, there's turnover of 17%—that many manufacturers merge, go bankrupt, or even evolve into a different kind of firm under another name.

Until fairly recently, garment manufacturers usually had their own factories on the premises.

Today, most firms use contractors—companies that don't design but manufacture only.

Methods of production vary considerably, according to the firm's price range. At couture houses like Norell, garments are made individually —usually, by the hands of a total of only four people, with one of them doing the bulk of the work. Upper-priced non-couture houses and their contractors use more machine work in production, but their workers are still highly-skilled— each, capable of making a garment from neckline to hemline; and usually, again, only three or four of them work on each garment.

Inexpensive houses operate quite differently. They or their contractors often go in for assembly-line production, called section work, with one person to sew hemlines, another for button-holes,

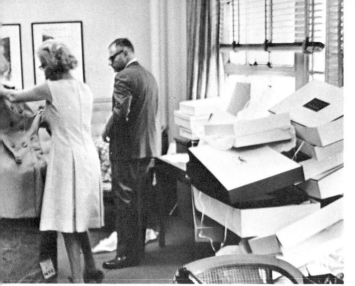

Macy's (N.Y.) buyers unpacking Paris originals.

another for collars, and so on. This work obviously, isn't as highly-skilled, so there isn't the same compelling need to stay close to New York, to be able to tap its pool of trained labor. Styles usually change more slowly in budget fashions, too; the manufacturer doesn't need a factory on the spot that can whip new styles into production as soon as a fresh fashion trend seems to be catching on. Consequently, lower-priced houses often give their work to factories outside the city or even in another state as far away as New England or the South, while medium and high-priced houses use contractors located in the garment center itself.

The route an idea follows as it passes down through the industry is interesting. When a leading designer, like Norell, shows a collection, makers of higher-priced lines watch the reactions to it eagerly. If they spot a style they think will sell at their own price-level, they adapt it. If the adaption does sell well, it will probably be imitated again by lower-priced firms, and perhaps still again, with the price sinking once again, until eventually something remotely like the Norell original can be found in the stores for $10. The $10 dress is made by "knock-off" houses in "Chinatown"—as Seventh Avenue calls 35th Street. The end result of this whole process for American society is that at every income level women can look well-dressed and even highly fashionable. Sociologists have pointed out that the poor in America are hard to identify, because good, inexpensive clothing is so easily available.

Upper-priced firms adapt and copy styles shown in Paris collections. Many manufacturers and their designers attend the openings. Since the collections are surrounded by secrecy, this can be done by invitation only, and arrivals are carefully screened to make sure their invitations are valid. Manufacturers and store buyers who intend to buy from a collection for resale and for copying are asked to make a deposit to guarantee a minimum purchase and the amount required runs as high as $1,000 at some houses. Some manufacturers buy only toiles, the design made up in muslin. An American store buyer, selecting a style to be copied, will bring it back and have the work done by one of the higher-priced American manufacturers. Originals and copies both appear in U.S. stores within a remarkably short time after the openings, but sometimes even before they arrive, Seventh Avenue houses will have begun to adapt some of the new ideas from Paris, as they were reported in newspapers and magazines.

Parisian fashions aren't the only ones that make their influence felt along Seventh Avenue. Besides the fashion industries of England, Spain, Italy, there are new ones now in other parts of the world, particularly in the Far East. Lord and Taylor, for example, imports clothes by Design-Thai. Jacquelin Ayer, a New York-born Jamaican, is the talent behind this Bangkok-based concern. She designs both fashions and the fabrics she makes them in. Until she began designing and wearing clothes that were adaptations of Thailand's traditional costumes, Thai socialites studiously avoided anything that looked as if it were native to their country. Other Far East designers who are becoming known here are Nakamura and Hanae Mori of Japan, and Marie Ah You of Tahiti.

Four outfits that glow are by Diana Dew for Paraphenalia, a New York City boutique. They light up when a button is pushed.

THE FUTURE

ALTHOUGH most garment firms are small, there's been a trend to bigness in the last four or five years. The new giants of the industry are Jonathan Logan and Bobbie Brooks. Both do in the neighborhood of a hundred million dollars worth of business each year, as compared to the rest of the industry, where most firms do less than a million dollars worth. Bobbie Brooks, thoroughly modern, goes in for market research, and uses computers to predict new fashion trends.

There are certain advantages to bigness. The large firm uses assembly-line production, and thus, dispenses with the need for highly skilled labor, so it can settle outside New York City, where rents, labor costs and taxes are lower. It maintains a huge force of salesmen, who go out and contact buyers, rather than waiting for buyers to come to them. It can afford to advertise, to make its name known. It makes several lines under different price ranges, so that if one collec-

tion fails, another is certain to pull the company through. It can buy fabrics in quantity and pay less for them because of the size of the order, and fabrics left over from one line, in one season, can always be used in another line the next. The fabric manufacturers, for the most part, are giants themselves and they prefer to deal in huge quantities. With the recent trend to shopping centers and branch stores which operate from a central office that buys in quantity, giant firms that can sell in quantity have acquired another advantage. They also won't have to cope with the gradual dwindling of the supply of trained factory hands and tailors that faces the rest of the industry, now that the influx of skilled immigrants from Europe has practically stopped.

Another trend has been the international concept—the Seventh Avenue firm, Malcom Starr, has headquarters in Zurich, Hong Kong and New York. They do business with England, Germany,

Inventory Control, Execumatic.

Upper East side New York City boutique, Serendipity.

Switzerland and Japan. Though there are national differences in taste, they all like the American way of fit, workmanship and style. In Japan the Gino Charles petite collection is most successful because of the oriental woman's small figure. The firm's designers have to think on an international basis. Malcolm Starr's volume for 1966 (which includes their subdivision, Gino Charles) was 14 million dollars—plus about 12 million in international sales. Besides a Director of Design and a Co-ordinator of Production, the firm of Malcolm Starr has a new member of the team—a machine for round-the-world inventory.

On the other hand, there's been a development in the opposite direction, away from bigness, in the growth of the off-Seventh Avenue wholesale firms. These were encouraged by the emergence, over the last ten years, of boutiques—small shops (or shops within big department stores) that sell offbeat few-of-a-kind fashions. More recently there has been a boutique explosion all over the world. In Paris it has been noted that St. Laurent has expressed more interest in his boutique than couture—Dior is opening a Miss Dior Boutique and Madame Grès and Cardin also have plans for boutiques. In Manhattan in 1966, according to the New York City Planning Commission, thirty-five boutiques opened in the upper Madison Avenue area alone—some of these highly individualized shops are even opening second stores. Almost all of them are full of fun and fantasy reflecting the avante-garde fashions of New York, London and Paris. Because of the creative freedom and offbeat styling, they have provided an excellent starting-off place for the beginning designer to market her ideas. The off-Seventh Avenue wholesale firms are either owned and run by the designer or she has a backer who lets her do as she pleases. Like artists, most of these young designers start in cheap lofts with nothing much in the way of assets except belief in themselves and their talent—and the knowledge that they do *not* want to make commercial clothes. The firms are purposely kept small, so that one person can easily control all facets of the operation. Most off-Seventh Avenue people, when they started, couldn't afford to buy from the big fabric houses and the regular lines of fabrics, but had to pick up odd pieces, a little at a time. This is still one of the chief characteristics of this kind of fashion: unusual fabrics which arrive on the market in small quantities. Another characteristic is that, although the clothes are factory-made, they usually have custom details such as printed china silk linings, hand-sewn seams, handsome closings, snaps on linings, as well as on the outer fabric. The California garment industry is like off-Seventh Avenue in that many firms—large ones, too—are designer-owned. Many of the great couture houses of New York are also owned, or partly owned, by the designer —more now than in the past. Examples are Bill Blass of Maurice Rentner, Norell, Trigère, Geoffrey Beene and Donald Brooks.

Mia Fonssagrives and Vickie Tiel designing at home.

St. Laurent

 Chanel

Cardin

 Marc Bohan

 Balenciaga

PARIS
COUTURE
DESIGNERS

LIVING

WITH THE

UPS &

DOWNS

…di Gernreich

Trigère

Norell

Bill Blass

Bonnie Cashin

Geoffrey Beene

ENERGY and enthusiasm are two of the most important qualities a young designer can have, according to a world-famous couturier. People in the fashion industry, he said, are impressed by real showmanship, and by the kind of person who has a strong drive to create.

Equally important, according to another fashion expert, is not letting yourself be talked into taking a job until you feel you're ready for it, and being willing to start at the bottom and learn. For a designer, talent is a prerequisite, of course, and earning a degree in the field is often the first step in a career. The talent is then tempered by on-the-job experience. Gradually, the young designer develops a sure sense of timing, and the confidence to stand by her instincts when she *knows* they're right. Gradually, she finds herself and her own niche as she really begins to grow as a designer.

A designer's career is bound to have ups and downs. Even today's most famous couturiers had some disappointments in the years when they were starting out. Just as a director in the theater can't expect to guide a hit every time, a designer must learn to take the occasional downs with the ups—and to look at both with perspective and a sense of humor.

Galanos

Donald Brooks

Jacques Tiffeau

BIBLIOGRAPHY

BOOKS

Crawford, M. D. C., Josephine Watkins, and Beatrice
Zelin (ed.). *One World of Fashion,* third edition.
New York: Fairchild Publications, Inc., 1967.

Helfgott, Roy B., W. Eric Gustafson, James M. Hund,
and Max Hall (ed.). *Made in New York.* Cam-
bridge, Massachusetts: Harvard University Press,
1959.

Jensen, Oliver. *The Revolt of American Woman.* New
York: Harcourt, Brace and Company, 1952.

Kaplan, Albert A., Margaret De Mille. *Careers in
Department Store Merchandising.* New York:
Henry Z. Walck, 1962.

Klapper, Marvin. *Fabric Almanac.* New York: Fairchild Publications, Inc., 1966.

Laver, James. *Taste and Fashion.* London: George G.
Harrap and Company, Ltd., 1948.

Stuart, Jessie. *The American Fashion Industry.* Boston:
Simmons College, 1951.

Wingate, Isabel (ed.). *Fairchild's Dictionary of Textiles,*
fifth edition. New York: Fairchild Publications,
Inc., 1967.

Wingate, Isabel. *Textile Fabrics and Their Selection.*
Englewood Cliffs, New Jersey: Prentice Hall,
1964.

Zweig, Stefan. *Marie Antoinette.* Garden City, New
York: Garden City Publishing Co., 1933.

PERIODICALS, RELATED MATERIALS

"1898–1948 Fifty Years of Fashion," *Golden Anni-
versary of Fashion Official Jubilee Edition,* 1948.

"Public Tries on Paper-Clothing Fad for Size,"
Barmash, Isadore, *New York Times, January, 1967.*

"Seventh Avenue Goes to Wall Street," Forbes, July,
1964.

"The Story of Wool," *Wool Bureau, Inc.,* 1958.

"What is Silk?" International Silk Association, 1958.

Women's Wear Daily, Fairchild Publications, Inc.

PHOTOGRAPHY AND ILLUSTRATION CREDITS